MW00934566

THE WIN PHILOSOPHY QUOTE BOOK

200 Quotes to Inspire YOU to Winning Ways

COACH SHERRY WINN

"AMERICA'S #1 SPORTS LEADERSHIP SPEAKER"

Author of *Unleash the Winner within You: A Success Game Plan for Business, Leadership and Life*

Cover, Design and Interior Layout by Teagarden Designs

ISBN-13:978-1530100941
ISBN-10:1530100941

10% of all royalties are donated to:
The Yellowstone Wildlife Sanctuary whose mission
is the protection and conservation of the Yellowstone
ecosystem, wildlife, and natural habitats.

To discover more visit:
www.yellowstonewildlifesanctuary.com

I offer a special thank you to Lauretta Yantis who has supported and encouraged me to strive for my dreams.

THE IDEAL SPEAKER FOR YOUR NEXT EVENT!

Any organization that wants to invigorate, stimulate and rejuvenate their team members needs to hire Coach Winn for a keynote and/or seminar training!!

To Contact or Book Coach Winn to Speak:
Ucancreatesuccess LLC
1193 Nye Road, Fishtail, MT 59028
304-380-4398

coachwinn@coachwinnspeaks.com
www.coachwinnspeaks.com
www.facebook.com/coachwinnspeaks
www.twitter.com/coachwinnspeaks

ABOUT COACH WINN

Coach Sherry Winn is an in-demand motivational speaker, a leading success coach and seminar trainer, a two-time Olympian, a national championship basketball coach, and an Amazon best seller. She has written five books including, *"Unleash the Winner within You: A Success Game Plan for Business, Leadership and Life."* Thousands, from small business owners to athletic coaches to corporate executives, have enjoyed Coach Winn's powerful interactive and humorous WINNING presentations.

With over 34 years of practicing leadership as an elite athlete and collegiate basketball coach, Sherry is an expert on coaching leaders and team members to championship status. She has successfully taken people beyond their levels of comfort to "WIN" against competitors who were superior in talent, facilities and financial budgets. Through her WIN Philosophy™ and WINNER Principles™, she teaches leaders and team members to be victorious even when the odds appear to be insurmountable.

A recognized authority on leadership and team development, Coach Winn shares with you the WINNER Principles which will enable you to rejuvenate, invigorate and stimulate you and your team members to become agents of change.

Audiences rave about Coach Winn's ability to enthusiastically deliver messages woven into humorous stories which are applicable for individuals within all levels of organizations. A passionate, sought-after author, speaker and business consultant, Coach Winn is characterized by friends, colleagues and clients as one of the most benevolent, perceptive and influential individuals in the business today.

To find out more about Coach Winn's seminars, books, trainings, and coaching, or to inquire about Coach Winn's availability to speak, you can contact her office at:

Ucancreatessuccess LLC
1193 Nye Road
Fishtail, MT 59028
304-380-4398
www.coachwinnspeaks.com

THE WIN PHILOSOPHY QUOTE BOOK

200 Quotes to Inspire YOU to Winning Ways

The following quotes are meant to inspire you and drive you to action. Beside each quote is a place for you to note 3 action steps. Every day when you read a quote, take a moment to write down the action steps you will take to live the quote.

WINNERS

"The winners go toward what they want rather than avoiding what they don't want."

ACTION STEPS:

1. _____

2. _____

3. _____

WINNERS

"The secret to being a winner is having the faith that you were born a winner. Once you know that are a winner, you act on your knowledge."

 ACTION STEPS:

1. _____

2. _____

3. _____

WINNERS

"If you knew you were created in appreciation, love and admiration, you would act like a winner. Act as if you were created like a winner and know the way toward all you desire."

ACTION STEPS:

1. _____

2. _____

3. _____

WINNERS

"You are a winner when you feel completely loved and able to see the winner in all those around you."

ACTION STEPS:

1. _____

2. _____

3. _____

WINNERS

"When you meet other people, see the winner within them as you would want to see the winner within yourself. As you act toward others, you act toward yourself."

 ## ACTION STEPS:

1. _____

2. _____

3. _____

WINNERS

"When you declare you are not a winner, you are egotistical because you believe your opinion of yourself is greater than God's opinion of you."

 ACTION STEPS:

1. _____

2. _____

3. _____

WINNERS

"If you refute success, you once knew what it was. If you can admit you denied yourself success, you can also acknowledge you can undo your denial."

ACTION STEPS:

1. _____

2. _____

3. _____

WINNERS

"Winners have not ceased because you refused to see them. Love has not died because you refuted it. Peace has not been abandoned because you left it. Nothing has been lost but your ability to see."

ACTION STEPS:

1. _____

2. _____

3. _____

WINNERS

"A true winner remains humble among success."

ACTION STEPS:

1. _____

2. _____

3. _____

WINNERS

"Winning is not about competition; it is about discovering the winner within you."

1. _____

2. _____

3. _____

WINNERS

*"Determine today that you
will no longer deceive yourself.
Acknowledge the winner you
were meant to be."*

ACTION STEPS:

1. _____

2. _____

3. _____

WINNERS

"Winners are just people with vision, faith and discipline."

 ACTION STEPS:

1. _____

2. _____

3. _____

WINNERS

*"To discover your inner winner,
nourish the miracle you are."*

1. _____

2. _____

3. _____

WINNERS

"Becoming a winner does not mean conquering another; being a winner means conquering your fears of inadequacy, lack and unworthiness."

ACTION STEPS:

1. _____

2. _____

3. _____

WINNERS

"*Winning comes in many ways as does losing, and both come from the same place you.*"

ACTION STEPS:

1. _____

2. _____

3. _____

WINNERS

"Winners have no need for harming others, because they do not need to prove they are strong."

ACTION STEPS:

1. _____

2. _____

3. _____

WINNERS

"To unleash the winner within you, release the past and look without judgment upon yourself for what you did or did not do."

 ## ACTION STEPS:

1. _____

2. _____

3. _____

WINNERS

*"Winning is not an event;
it is a decision."*

ACTION STEPS:

1. _____

2. _____

3. _____

W:
WIDEN THE
SEPARATOR GAP

"If you want consistency in being your best, have consistency with the thought you are the best."

ACTION STEPS:

1. _____

2. _____

3. _____

W:
WIDEN THE
SEPARATOR GAP

"Winners come from all walks of life as do losers. What separates the winners from the losers has nothing to do with where they grew up; winning has to do with what attitude grew inside them."

ACTION STEPS:

1. _____

2. _____

3. _____

W:
WIDEN THE
SEPARATOR GAP

"There is no sometimes in total commitment. There is no fence nor line. You are either all in or all out."

 ACTION STEPS:

1. _____

2. _____

3. _____

W:
WIDEN THE
SEPARATOR GAP

"When you value a lie about yourself such as you are unworthy, you invest in that lie. Your lie remains true as long as you value your investment in it."

 ## ACTION STEPS:

1. _____

2. _____

3. _____

W:
WIDEN THE
SEPARATOR GAP

"To promote winning, you recognize your own worth. To help other people win, you value their worth."

ACTION STEPS:

1. _____

2. _____

3. _____

W:
WIDEN THE
SEPARATOR GAP

"Your whole purpose of learning is to break away from self-imposed boundaries."

ACTION STEPS:

1. _____

2. _____

3. _____

W:
WIDEN THE
SEPARATOR GAP

*"The faster you forgive
yourself for your mistakes,
the quicker you move toward
the success you desire."*

 ACTION STEPS:

1. _____

2. _____

3. _____

W:
WIDEN THE
SEPARATOR GAP

"Your choices are a reflection of your values. If you value failure, you choose to find events which support failure. If you value winning, you discover events which reinforce winning."

 ACTION STEPS:

1. _____

2. _____

3. _____

W:
WIDEN THE
SEPARATOR GAP

"When we seek the best within ourselves, we find it. When we judge ourselves, we find guilt which makes us small."

 **ACTION STEPS:**

1. _____

2. _____

3. _____

W:
WIDEN THE
SEPARATOR GAP

"Nothing is so loved as a goal which your mind accepts as truth."

 ## ACTION STEPS:

1. _____

2. _____

3. _____

W:
WIDEN THE
SEPARATOR GAP

"Being positive doesn't solve all your problems, but positivity does make working toward the answers feel better."

 ## ACTION STEPS:

1. _____

2. _____

3. _____

W:
WIDEN THE
SEPARATOR GAP

"If a goal is possible, then so are all the steps toward the goal. Take action now."

ACTION STEPS:

1. _____

2. _____

3. _____

W:
WIDEN THE
SEPARATOR GAP

*"How long do you repeat
an action to create a desired
habit? The answer: as long
as it takes. Otherwise it is not
important to you."*

ACTION STEPS:

1. _____

2. _____

3. _____

W:
WIDEN THE
SEPARATOR GAP

"What separates you from what you want is fear. Fear is not real; it is imagined through your lack of self-worth. To get what you want, work on who you are."

 ## ACTION STEPS:

1. _____

2. _____

3. _____

W:
WIDEN THE
SEPARATOR GAP

"When you get trapped in the belief that your thoughts are true, you cannot see past them."

 ## ACTION STEPS:

1. _____

2. _____

3. _____

W:
WIDEN THE
SEPARATOR GAP

*"When you have conviction
you will win your goals,
patience is easy."*

 ## ACTION STEPS:

1. _____

2. _____

3. _____

W:
WIDEN THE
SEPARATOR GAP

*"The delay in your desires is not
from somebody or something
else; the delay comes from the
separation between what you want
and where you are in your belief
that you can have it."*

ACTION STEPS:

1. _____

2. _____

3. _____

W:
WIDEN THE
SEPARATOR GAP

"The idea that pain is needed to reach a goal is equal to believing one must learn how to drown to enjoy the water."

ACTION STEPS:

1. _____

2. _____

3. _____

W:
WIDEN THE
SEPARATOR GAP

*"Every time you make a choice, it is
an evaluation of yourself."*

ACTION STEPS:

1. _____

2. _____

3. _____

W:
WIDEN THE
SEPARATOR GAP

"Blaming is responsible for failure because it holds you powerless to move forward."

ACTION STEPS:

1. _____

2. _____

3. _____

I:
IDENTIFY "I AM"
AS POWER WORDS

"I AM are your two most powerful words, because they determine your direction, your faith and your destination."

 ## ACTION STEPS:

1. _____

2. _____

3. _____

I:
IDENTIFY "I AM"
AS POWER WORDS

"What stops us is our inability to hear the limiting words we tell ourselves."

 ## ACTION STEPS:

1. _____

2. _____

3. _____

I:
IDENTIFY "I AM"
AS POWER WORDS

"Whatever you agree to in your thoughts becomes your truth. It is your acknowledgment of your thoughts which make them valid."

 ## ACTION STEPS:

1. _____

2. _____

3. _____

I:
IDENTIFY "I AM" AS POWER WORDS

"You respond to events through your thoughts of who you are. If you want your events to change, then change your interpretation of events."

ACTION STEPS:

1. _____

2. _____

3. _____

I:
IDENTIFY "I AM" AS POWER WORDS

"What you want to be is inescapably tied to who you think you are."

 ACTION STEPS:

1. _____

2. _____

3. _____

I:
IDENTIFY "I AM"
AS POWER WORDS

"Belief is acceptance and disbelief is rejection. You choose to live through either faith or fear receiving life through your beliefs."

 ## ACTION STEPS:

1. _____

2. _____

3. _____

I:
IDENTIFY "I AM"
AS POWER WORDS

"Nothing beyond yourself can make you feel immense or trivial, because all thoughts are yours."

 ## ACTION STEPS:

1. _____

2. _____

3. _____

I:
IDENTIFY "I AM"
AS POWER WORDS

"When you criticize yourself, it is an indication that you hate who you think you are."

ACTION STEPS:

1. _____

2. _____

3. _____

I:
IDENTIFY "I AM"
AS POWER WORDS

"Whatever story you tell yourself becomes your truth. Switch your story to create a better outcome."

 ACTION STEPS:

1. _____

2. _____

3. _____

I:
IDENTIFY "I AM"
AS POWER WORDS

"When you focus on your goodness, you are in alignment with who you really are."

ACTION STEPS:

1. _____

2. _____

3. _____

I:
IDENTIFY "I AM"
AS POWER WORDS

"Once you decide you are responsible for what you see, you can choose the life you want to live."

 ## ACTION STEPS:

1. _____

2. _____

3. _____

I:
IDENTIFY "I AM"
AS POWER WORDS

"Everybody gives and receives, and you can only receive what you want and give who you are."

 ACTION STEPS:

1. _____

2. _____

3. _____

I:
IDENTIFY "I AM"
AS POWER WORDS

"The biggest boost to self-esteem is the awareness that you don't have to carry guilt."

ACTION STEPS:

1. _____

2. _____

3. _____

I:
IDENTIFY "I AM"
AS POWER WORDS

"If you want your life to change, change yourself. You are in the driver's seat."

ACTION STEPS:

1. _____

2. _____

3. _____

I:
IDENTIFY "I AM"
AS POWER WORDS

"Be ever vigilant of those people who try to convince you of who you are, because your perception of you determines the reality of the world you choose to live in."

 **ACTION STEPS:**

1. _____

2. _____

3. _____

I:
IDENTIFY "I AM"
AS POWER WORDS

*"When we get stuck in
the definition of ourselves, we
cannot see our possibilities."*

ACTION STEPS:

1. _____

2. _____

3. _____

I:
IDENTIFY "I AM"
AS POWER WORDS

"When you have a personal investment in a situation, you cannot dislodge your judgment from the situation. You see who you are and thus the situation becomes what you want it to be."

ACTION STEPS:

1. _____

2. _____

3. _____

I:
IDENTIFY "I AM"
AS POWER WORDS

"We ask for positive words from others that we deny ourselves, and become angry when they refuse to give positive words to us. Why would they give us what refuse to offer ourselves?"

 **ACTION STEPS:**

1. _____

2. _____

3. _____

I:
IDENTIFY "I AM"
AS POWER WORDS

"Be careful what you think about yourself, because thoughts are real. Thoughts appear first as energy before manifesting as things."

 ACTION STEPS:

1. _____

2. _____

3. _____

I:
IDENTIFY "I AM"
AS POWER WORDS

"If you compare yourself with others, you must perceive yourself as weak, because only the weak need to prove their strength."

ACTION STEPS:

1. _____

2. _____

3. _____

N:
NAVIGATE
SUCCESS

"Believe you are deprived of nothing, and you are prepared to receive everything."

 ## ACTION STEPS:

1. _____

2. _____

3. _____

N:
NAVIGATE
SUCCESS

"The idea of scarcity keeps us confined to the belief that if another gains, we lose."

ACTION STEPS:

1. _____

2. _____

3. _____

N:
NAVIGATE
SUCCESS

*"When you open yourself up
to being a learn-it-all, teachers
become available."*

 ACTION STEPS:

1. _____

2. _____

3. _____

N:
NAVIGATE
SUCCESS

"You destroy your motivation for learning when you think you already know."

ACTION STEPS:

1. _____

2. _____

3. _____

N:
NAVIGATE SUCCESS

"When you learn that miracles are possible for you, you stop fighting the idea of them."

 ## ACTION STEPS:

1. _____

2. _____

3. _____

N:
NAVIGATE
SUCCESS

"Knowledge is not power; utilizing your knowledge is power."

 ## ACTION STEPS:

1. _____

2. _____

3. _____

N:
NAVIGATE
SUCCESS

"The only obstacle preventing you from success is your belief in the truth of the limitations you set for yourself."

 ACTION STEPS:

1. _____

2. _____

3. _____

N:
NAVIGATE
SUCCESS

"The essential piece of wisdom missing in most people is the acknowledgment of what they do not know."

 ACTION STEPS:

1. _____

2. _____

3. _____

N:
NAVIGATE
SUCCESS

"You distort your thinking by maintaining two systems of opposite beliefs. You cannot know success and know failure for each denies the other."

 ACTION STEPS:

1. _____

2. _____

3. _____

N:
NAVIGATE
SUCCESS

"There is no guilt in learning for lessons are not mistakes."

 **ACTION STEPS:**

1. _____

2. _____

3. _____

N:
NAVIGATE
SUCCESS

"When you offer blessings to another, you have accepted the blessing for yourself. For how can you give away gifts you do not know?"

 ## ACTION STEPS:

1. _____

2. _____

3. _____

www.CoachWinnSpeaks.com

N:
NAVIGATE
SUCCESS

*"All perceived failure is a delusion
of the ego for failure is the belief
you have not gained from
the experience."*

 ACTION STEPS:

1. _____

2. _____

3. _____

N:
NAVIGATE
SUCCESS

*"Knowing your purpose
is your power."*

 ACTION STEPS:

1. _____

2. _____

3. _____

N:
NAVIGATE
SUCCESS

"Those people who value success value themselves first."

 ACTION STEPS:

1. _____

2. _____

3. _____

N:
NAVIGATE
SUCCESS

"Look first inside yourself for the answer. It is there waiting for you to acknowledge."

 ACTION STEPS:

1. _____

2. _____

3. _____

www.CoachWinnSpeaks.com

N:
NAVIGATE
SUCCESS

"Assume the best and you will find the best, because you find the answers you search for."

 ## ACTION STEPS:

1. _____

2. _____

3. _____

N:
NAVIGATE
SUCCESS

"When you focus on failure, you become helpless. Why not focus on faith, courage and independence?"

 ACTION STEPS:

1. _____

2. _____

3. _____

N:
NAVIGATE
SUCCESS

"Some of your greatest achievements you have called failures. Know all things are for your highest good."

ACTION STEPS:

1. _____

2. _____

3. _____

N:
NAVIGATE
SUCCESS

"Your mind is capable of dreaming all things, and the mind can also deny the dreams it created."

ACTION STEPS:

1. _____

2. _____

3. _____

N:
NAVIGATE
SUCCESS

"When you desire a goal and fear that you will not obtain your goal, you are not ready to receive it."

 ACTION STEPS:

1. _____

2. _____

3. _____

W:
WELCOME YOUR
CHALLENGES

*"How you respond to a person or
an event is your interpretation of
the event. Your interpretation is
only your truth."*

 ACTION STEPS:

1. _____

2. _____

3. _____

W:
WELCOME YOUR
CHALLENGES

*"Being thankful is a mindset.
Thankfulness arrives by looking for
the good in all situations."*

ACTION STEPS:

1. _____

2. _____

3. _____

W:
WELCOME YOUR CHALLENGES

"We are all creators of our lives. Why some people choose to create misery and others choose to create happiness is directly related to how empowered they feel."

 ACTION STEPS:

1. _____

2. _____

3. _____

W:
WELCOME YOUR CHALLENGES

"You choose every day which way you want to walk. You can turn toward happiness, success and peace or toward anger, poverty and misery."

 **ACTION STEPS:**

1. _____

2. _____

3. _____

W:
WELCOME YOUR CHALLENGES

"When you believe in the impossible, your belief is the result of your thought the impossible can happen."

 ## ACTION STEPS:

1. _____

2. _____

3. _____

W:
WELCOME YOUR CHALLENGES

"Only the people who believe in miracles live them."

 ## ACTION STEPS:

1. _____

2. _____

3. _____

W:
WELCOME YOUR CHALLENGES

"Every challenge becomes what you want the challenge to be. The challenge can enrich you or defeat you."

ACTION STEPS:

1. _____

2. _____

3. _____

W:
WELCOME YOUR CHALLENGES

"Most of your misery comes from the belief you are powerless to create the dreams you desire."

ACTION STEPS:

1. _____

2. _____

3. _____

W:
WELCOME YOUR
CHALLENGES

"When you forgive, you let go of the need to remember. You move beyond the past giving the past no power over you."

ACTION STEPS:

1. _____

2. _____

3. _____

www.CoachWinnSpeaks.com

W:
WELCOME YOUR CHALLENGES

"You cannot separate yourself from your challenges. You experience the challenge because of who you are."

 ACTION STEPS:

1. _____

2. _____

3. _____

W:
WELCOME YOUR CHALLENGES

"Where does fear originate if not within yourself? To overcome fear, then, is to learn to value and trust who you are."

 ACTION STEPS:

1. _____

2. _____

3. _____

W:
WELCOME YOUR CHALLENGES

"You cannot see what you do not believe; therefore, in order to overcome a challenge, you work on your belief the challenge can be achieved."

 ACTION STEPS:

1. _____

2. _____

3. _____

W:
WELCOME YOUR
CHALLENGES

"Sometimes we get stuck in the challenge, because we aren't convinced we are ready for the answer."

 ACTION STEPS:

1. _____

2. _____

3. _____

W:
WELCOME YOUR
CHALLENGES

*"It is easy to help the individual
who challenges answers for she
recognizes she cannot know
all the answers."*

 ACTION STEPS:

1. _____

2. _____

3. _____

W:
WELCOME YOUR CHALLENGES

"How you view challenges in the world has a reference point within you. Your perception determines true or false, good or bad, and right or wrong."

ACTION STEPS:

1. _____

2. _____

3. _____

W:
WELCOME YOUR
CHALLENGES

*"Once you understand the answer
is within you, you don't have
to search for the answer
anywhere else."*

ACTION STEPS:

1. _____

2. _____

3. _____

W:
WELCOME YOUR
CHALLENGES

"When you look at challenges as lessons about life, you accept each challenge as a gift."

 ACTION STEPS:

1. _____

2. _____

3. _____

www.CoachWinnSpeaks.com

W:
WELCOME YOUR CHALLENGES

"If you desire peace, abandon judgment about your challenges."

 ACTION STEPS:

1. _____

2. _____

3. _____

W:
WELCOME YOUR CHALLENGES

"To judge yourself on how you meet your challenges is failure to learn from your challenges."

 ## ACTION STEPS:

1. _____

2. _____

3. _____

W:
WELCOME YOUR
CHALLENGES

"Your self-worth is a product of how you meet your challenges."

 ACTION STEPS:

1. _____

2. _____

3. _____

I:
IMPROVE YOUR
COMMUNICATION

*"Words meant to harm tell
more about the speaker than
the receiver of the words."*

 ACTION STEPS:

1. _____

2. _____

3. _____

I:
IMPROVE YOUR COMMUNICATION

"When you offer sympathy, you give pity. When you offer empathy, you give understanding and hope."

 ## ACTION STEPS:

1. _____

2. _____

3. _____

I:
IMPROVE YOUR COMMUNICATION

"When you use your words to empower others, you become empowered."

ACTION STEPS:

1. _____

2. _____

3. _____

I:
IMPROVE YOUR
COMMUNICATION

*"We tend to live our words
so watch the words you
whisper in your ear."*

 ACTION STEPS:

1. _____

2. _____

3. _____

I:
IMPROVE YOUR
COMMUNICATION

"When you listen to other people, remember their words are representation of the experiences they've had."

 ## ACTION STEPS:

1. _____

2. _____

3. _____

I:
IMPROVE YOUR
COMMUNICATION

"Ignorance is represented by words
which are meant to demean,
demoralize and destroy."

 ## ACTION STEPS:

1. _____

2. _____

3. _____

I:
IMPROVE YOUR
COMMUNICATION

"Your responsibility in every conversation is to be present."

 ACTION STEPS:

1. _____

2. _____

3. _____

I:
IMPROVE YOUR COMMUNICATION

"What is more important than the words other people speak is your ability to see the intent of their words."

 ACTION STEPS:

1. _____

2. _____

3. _____

I:
IMPROVE YOUR
COMMUNICATION

*"Our words represent the journey
we have taken and the lessons
we have learned."*

ACTION STEPS:

1. _____

2. _____

3. _____

I:
IMPROVE YOUR
COMMUNICATION

"Before you speak, learn how your words can wound or heal others."

ACTION STEPS:

1. _____

2. _____

3. _____

I:
IMPROVE YOUR COMMUNICATION

"Every internal conversation you have with yourself brings you either closer or further away from love."

ACTION STEPS:

1. _____

2. _____

3. _____

I:
IMPROVE YOUR COMMUNICATION

"You can tell how much love people have for themselves by the way they listen without the need to be heard."

ACTION STEPS:

1. _____

2. _____

3. _____

I:
IMPROVE YOUR
COMMUNICATION

"Conflict is not a sign of poor communication; choosing to remain in conflict is."

 ## ACTION STEPS:

1. _____

2. _____

3. _____

www.CoachWinnSpeaks.com

I:
IMPROVE YOUR COMMUNICATION

"If you want to truly hear what other people have to say, let them know you stand free of judgment."

 ACTION STEPS:

1. _____

2. _____

3. _____

I:
IMPROVE YOUR
COMMUNICATION

*"Conversations should convey
your belief that you are worthy
of hearing what the other
person has to share."*

 ## ACTION STEPS:

1. _____

2. _____

3. _____

I:
IMPROVE YOUR COMMUNICATION

> *"In every conversation, seek first what you can give."*

 ## ACTION STEPS:

1. _____

2. _____

3. _____

I:
IMPROVE YOUR
COMMUNICATION

"For people to hear you, they must believe you offer more than words. You must first offer compassion."

 ACTION STEPS:

1. _____

2. _____

3. _____

I:
IMPROVE YOUR
COMMUNICATION

"Your words are delivered through your voice, heart and mind. Your words are delivered through the essence of you."

 ## ACTION STEPS:

1. _____

2. _____

3. _____

I:
IMPROVE YOUR COMMUNICATION

"In a world where change is constant, honest communication is not only essential; honest communication is critical."

 ACTION STEPS:

1. _____

2. _____

3. _____

I:
IMPROVE YOUR
COMMUNICATION

*"Our external language is
a reflection of our internal truths."*

 ## ACTION STEPS:

1. _____

2. _____

3. _____

N:
NURTURE YOUR RELATIONSHIPS

"When you deny others love, you deny yourself love. What you withhold from others, you withhold from yourself."

 ACTION STEPS:

1. _____

2. _____

3. _____

N:
NURTURE YOUR
RELATIONSHIPS

*"You cannot offer what you
don't have and you cannot
teach what you do not know.
Be wary then of the people
who offer the way toward love
while condemning others."*

 ACTION STEPS:

1. _____

2. _____

3. _____

N:
NURTURE YOUR
RELATIONSHIPS

"If you attack somebody else, you attack because you believe you are deprived. There is no reason to attack when you feel whole."

 ## ACTION STEPS:

1. _____

2. _____

3. _____

N:
NURTURE YOUR
RELATIONSHIPS

"Perpetuating judgments about others illuminates and disseminates those judgments back upon you."

 ACTION STEPS:

1. _____

2. _____

3. _____

N:
NURTURE YOUR
RELATIONSHIPS

"It is not your job to change your brothers, sisters or neighbors. It is your job to accept and love them."

 ACTION STEPS:

1. _____

2. _____

3. _____

N:
NURTURE YOUR
RELATIONSHIPS

"When you criticize others, you deny yourself. You deny yourself of your own good while you defend your criticism."

 ACTION STEPS:

1. _____

2. _____

3. _____

N:
NURTURE YOUR
RELATIONSHIPS

"There is no judgment of others without telling a story about yourself."

 ## ACTION STEPS:

1. _____

2. _____

3. _____

N:
NURTURE YOUR RELATIONSHIPS

"We are completed through our ability to unconditionally love ourselves and others."

ACTION STEPS:

1. _____

2. _____

3. _____

N:
NURTURE YOUR RELATIONSHIPS

"How do we help others? We offer acceptance rather judgment."

 ACTION STEPS:

1. _____

2. _____

3. _____

N:
NURTURE YOUR
RELATIONSHIPS

"When communicating with others, understand they speak from their experiences and their experiences determine their perceptions. Their perceptions in turn, create their beliefs."

ACTION STEPS:

1. _____

2. _____

3. _____

N:
NURTURE YOUR
RELATIONSHIPS

"If you want others to obey you, you are requesting they submit to you. What does this say about your ego?"

ACTION STEPS:

1. _____

2. _____

3. _____

N:
NURTURE YOUR
RELATIONSHIPS

"Judging what you do not understand is an error and to pretend you understand another person is an even bigger error."

ACTION STEPS:

1. _____

2. _____

3. _____

N:
NURTURE YOUR
RELATIONSHIPS

"If you want other people to see the good in you, see the good in them."

 ACTION STEPS:

1. _____

2. _____

3. _____

N:
NURTURE YOUR RELATIONSHIPS

"Whenever you become angry with another, for whatever reason, your ego is in charge of your emotions. The attack you seek will not rectify the discord within you."

ACTION STEPS:

1. _____

2. _____

3. _____

N:
NURTURE YOUR
RELATIONSHIPS

"Your belief that punishing another frees you is the same belief that prevents you from joy."

 ## ACTION STEPS:

1. _____

2. _____

3. _____

N:
NURTURE YOUR
RELATIONSHIPS

"All people that you condemn keep your words and cherish your words so much that they hold your condemnation and return it to you."

ACTION STEPS:

1. _____

2. _____

3. _____

N:
NURTURE YOUR
RELATIONSHIPS

"By rejecting the condemnation of others, you free not only yourself; you teach others their words are harmless."

 **ACTION STEPS:**

1. _____

2. _____

3. _____

N:
NURTURE YOUR RELATIONSHIPS

"To judge others who have not yet reached awareness is your failure to learn from them."

 ## ACTION STEPS:

1. _____

2. _____

3. _____

N:
NURTURE YOUR RELATIONSHIPS

"The definition of abuse: when you use others to support your ego."

ACTION STEPS:

1. _____

2. _____

3. _____

N:
NURTURE YOUR RELATIONSHIPS

"When you accept others rather than trying to change them, you create the change you wish to see."

ACTION STEPS:

1. _____

2. _____

3. _____

N:
NOURISH
YOURSELF

"We have been taught that to love is dangerous—that love puts us at risk for vulnerability. The truth is that not to love is the danger. Without love we are empty and have nothing to give."

ACTION STEPS:

1. _____

2. _____

3. _____

N:
NOURISH
YOURSELF

"Fear is your tie to the belief that you are not worthy."

ACTION STEPS:

1. _____

2. _____

3. _____

N:
NOURISH
YOURSELF

"Judgment is what separates us from unconditional love."

 ## ACTION STEPS:

1. _____

2. _____

3. _____

N:
NOURISH
YOURSELF

"Once you understand love is within you, you don't have to search for it anywhere else."

ACTION STEPS:

1. _____

2. _____

3. _____

N:
NOURISH
YOURSELF

"Blaming others is an attack against yourself for it holds you prisoner to your current status."

ACTION STEPS:

1. _____

2. _____

3. _____

N:
NOURISH
YOURSELF

"You cannot perceive part of yourself as disgusting and believe you are at peace."

 ## ACTION STEPS:

1. _____

2. _____

3. _____

N:
NOURISH
YOURSELF

"Whatever you conceal from yourself keeps you from loving all of you."

 ## ACTION STEPS:

1. _____

2. _____

3. _____

N:
NOURISH
YOURSELF

"Your ego is that part of you which leads you toward insecurity and urges you to act out of fear rather than love. Your higher self is that part of you which answers only in love and faith."

ACTION STEPS:

1. _____

2. _____

3. _____

N:
NOURISH
YOURSELF

*"You cannot extract yourself
from the lies you tell yourself
until you admit your lies, because
denying them is the way your lies
are protected."*

 **ACTION STEPS:**

1. _____

2. _____

3. _____

N:
NOURISH
YOURSELF

"Conceit is the dismissal of love, because love contributes and conceit suppresses."

1. _____

2. _____

3. _____

N:
NOURISH
YOURSELF

"Guilt is the act of punishing yourself repeatedly for an event which already has taken place."

 ## ACTION STEPS:

1. _____

2. _____

3. _____

N:
NOURISH
YOURSELF

"Your ability to learn is only limited by your determination to learn."

ACTION STEPS:

1. _____

2. _____

3. _____

N:
NOURISH
YOURSELF

"When you project your illusions of insecurity, scarcity and inability to other people, you do not get rid of them. You grow them bigger within yourself."

ACTION STEPS:

1. _____

2. _____

3. _____

N:
NOURISH
YOURSELF

"Bury your ideas that love is not powerful enough. It is. Love alters lives beginning with your own."

 ACTION STEPS:

1. _____

2. _____

3. _____

N:
NOURISH
YOURSELF

*"When you hold back love,
you withhold love both from
yourself and others."*

 **ACTION STEPS:**

1. _____

2. _____

3. _____

N:
NOURISH
YOURSELF

"The biggest boost to self-esteem is the awareness that you don't have to carry guilt."

ACTION STEPS:

1. _____

2. _____

3. _____

N-NOURISH YOURSELF

"All of us are leaders in some way or another and great leaders build people. Your job, then, is to build yourself."

 ACTION STEPS:

1. _____

2. _____

3. _____

N-NOURISH YOURSELF

"We prevent ourselves from love through our judgment. The answer is forgiveness. "

 ACTION STEPS:

1. _____

2. _____

3. _____

N:
NOURISH
YOURSELF

"Judgment is easy because we practice judging all our lives. The challenge for us is to let go of judgment and allow love to take its place."

ACTION STEPS:

1. _____

2. _____

3. _____

N:
NOURISH
YOURSELF

"To recognize what does not matter allows you to focus on what is important. We waste our time on the trivial while ignoring the essential—that loving ourselves is the most crucial task at hand."

ACTION STEPS:

1. _____

2. _____

3. _____

E:
EXPECT
THE BEST

*"Happiness comes from
the consistent desire to be happy
and then to see and live in
the events which make you happy."*

ACTION STEPS:

1. _____

2. _____

3. _____

E:
EXPECT
THE BEST

"If you expect great events in your life and talk about them as if they are real, you cannot live without the evidence of those events."

 **ACTION STEPS:**

1. _____

2. _____

3. _____

E:
EXPECT
THE BEST

"You cannot separate yourself from the praise or condemnation you give to others. You are what you give."

ACTION STEPS:

1. _____

2. _____

3. _____

E:
EXPECT
THE BEST

"There is no separation between giving and receiving so receive and give freely."

ACTION STEPS:

1. _____

2. _____

3. _____

E:
EXPECT
THE BEST

*"Some people don't believe in magic.
I do...which is why I experience
magic every day."*

 ## ACTION STEPS:

1. _____

2. _____

3. _____

E:
EXPECT
THE BEST

"We possess more control than imagined. Every time we make an excuse we control our destiny."

ACTION STEPS:

1. _____

2. _____

3. _____

E:
EXPECT
THE BEST

"Your control your perspective which is your reality. To change your reality, alter your perspective."

ACTION STEPS:

1. _____

2. _____

3. _____

E:
EXPECT
THE BEST

"When we live in complete forgiveness of ourselves and others, we change the world."

ACTION STEPS:

1. _____

2. _____

3. _____

E:
EXPECT
THE BEST

"Your belief you can harbor both guilt and innocence is an illusion. Whichever emotion you choose determines how you occupy happiness."

 **ACTION STEPS:**

1. _____

2. _____

3. _____

E:
EXPECT
THE BEST

"Whenever you are attracted to the idea of suffering, remember the concept that when you decide upon suffering, you have let go of happiness."

ACTION STEPS:

1. _____

2. _____

3. _____

E:
EXPECT
THE BEST

"All real progress comes from your courage to look inside yourself and change what is not in alignment with love."

 ## ACTION STEPS:

1. _____

2. _____

3. _____

E:
EXPECT
THE BEST

"We find hatred easy to give and love hard to accept. Is this because we associate hatred with power and love with frailty?"

ACTION STEPS:

1. _____

2. _____

3. _____

E:
EXPECT
THE BEST

"Self-esteem comes from personal growth, which is built brick by brick by extending love throughout yourself and to others."

 **ACTION STEPS:**

1. _____

2. _____

3. _____

E:
EXPECT
THE BEST

"When you realize all the hurt you perceive begins in your own mind, you have identified the source, and have the ability to stop the hurt where it originates."

 **ACTION STEPS:**

1. _____

2. _____

3. _____

E:
EXPECT
THE BEST

"When you identify with emotions which belittle, demean or demoralize others, you deprive yourself of love."

 ## ACTION STEPS:

1. _____

2. _____

3. _____

E:
EXPECT
THE BEST

"Fear is the answer to what is not believed. To find faith, search for the belief which you have denied."

 ACTION STEPS:

1. _____

2. _____

3. _____

E:
EXPECT
THE BEST

*"When you respond to somebody
else's perception about you,
you give them power over you."*

ACTION STEPS:

1. _____

2. _____

3. _____

E:
EXPECT
THE BEST

"You don't respond to events directly; you respond to your story about them. Your story becomes your justification for your reaction."

 ACTION STEPS:

1. _____

2. _____

3. _____

E:
EXPECT
THE BEST

"When you set limits on what you believe you can do, you limit not only yourself but those who would benefit from your gifts."

 ACTION STEPS:

1. _____

2. _____

3. _____

www.CoachWinnSpeaks.com

E:
EXPECT
THE BEST

*"Empowerment is
the recognition that the force
to create opportunities is
within us. It is us."*

ACTION STEPS:

1. _____

2. _____

3. _____

R:
RECOVER
FROM THE PAST

*"When you can view your past
as a blessing rather than a curse,
you can stand in the present
and seek your future."*

 **ACTION STEPS:**

1. _____

2. _____

3. _____

R:
RECOVER
FROM THE PAST

"When you rehearse your stories about the past, you create your belief systems about the future."

ACTION STEPS:

1. _____

2. _____

3. _____

R:
RECOVER
FROM THE PAST

*"If you believe you must learn
a lesson before you let go of your
past, you are held to the past.
What if the lesson was to
release the past?"*

ACTION STEPS:

1. _____

2. _____

3. _____

R:
RECOVER
FROM THE PAST

"Every day is a new day except when we hold onto the past and allow it to interrupt the present."

 ACTION STEPS:

1. _____

2. _____

3. _____

R:
RECOVER
FROM THE PAST

"Our past is the major obstacle we have in front of us which prevents us from reaching our dreams."

 ## ACTION STEPS:

1. _____

2. _____

3. _____

R:
RECOVER
FROM THE PAST

*"Tomorrow repeats as today
when you give your past
permission to stay with you."*

ACTION STEPS:

1. _____

2. _____

3. _____

R:
RECOVER
FROM THE PAST

"What pieces of your past do you hold onto—the pleasant or the painful? Why do you choose to remember the painful past and how many times do you have to relive it to let it go?"

ACTION STEPS:

1. _____

2. _____

3. _____

R:
RECOVER
FROM THE PAST

"Your ego devotes most of its energy to the past and believes the past is the only facet of time which is noteworthy. Thus your ego prevents you from enjoying the present and believing in a superior future."

ACTION STEPS:

1. _____

2. _____

3. _____

R:
RECOVER
FROM THE PAST

"When you believe you can pay off your past through your future, the past determines your future by keeping you rooted in what once was."

 ACTION STEPS:

1. _____

2. _____

3. _____

R:
RECOVER
FROM THE PAST

*"The past has vanished and
to believe the past is still here
is to embed yourself in pain.
Your pain from what no longer
exists targets your present
and sabotages your future."*

 ACTION STEPS:

1. _____

2. _____

3. _____

R:
RECOVER
FROM THE PAST

"Your past events have no power over you unless you bring them forward with you to the present."

ACTION STEPS:

1. _____

2. _____

3. _____

R:
RECOVER
FROM THE PAST

"When you can look at all people with no reference to the past, either theirs or yours, you can see what is."

ACTION STEPS:

1. _____

2. _____

3. _____

R:
RECOVER
FROM THE PAST

"It might feel normal for you to use your past as a position to determine the future. Instead using your past is delusional, because the past no longer exists."

 ACTION STEPS:

1. _____

2. _____

3. _____

R:
RECOVER
FROM THE PAST

"Blame and disapproval are behind you unless you choose to align your present and future with them."

ACTION STEPS:

1. _____

2. _____

3. _____

R:
RECOVER
FROM THE PAST

"*Only your past can separate you from who you want to become and it is gone.*"

 ## ACTION STEPS:

1. _____

2. _____

3. _____

R:
RECOVER
FROM THE PAST

"When you live with guilt, you have made the decision to bring the past with you and to keep the past alive through your guilt."

 ACTION STEPS:

1. _____

2. _____

3. _____

R:
RECOVER
FROM THE PAST

"*The past that you remember
is altered by your wisdom.*"

 ACTION STEPS:

1. _____

2. _____

3. _____

www.CoachWinnSpeaks.com

R:
RECOVER
FROM THE PAST

*"What you learned is in the past;
the influence of what you
learned is forever."*

ACTION STEPS:

1. _____

2. _____

3. _____

R:
RECOVER
FROM THE PAST

"Nothing you learned can unravel the past; therefore, it is fruitless to try."

ACTION STEPS:

1. _____

2. _____

3. _____

R:
RECOVER
FROM THE PAST

*"Turning the past around
a thousand times does not grant
you greater insight. It does,
however, cause greater distress."*

ACTION STEPS:

1. _____

2. _____

3. _____

ONE MORE WINNING MESSAGE FOR YOU

Most people stop dreaming about their future because they become rooted in their past. Your past is over and completed. The past is not an indicator of your future unless you allow it to be.

I know you are one of the special people, the WINNERS in life, who choose to stop refreshing and rehashing your past events, who has forgiven yourself for whatever mistakes you've made, and who is now stretching your comfort zone to align with the miracle you came on earth to be.

My mission with the words I write and speak are to stimulate you to move beyond your self-perceived limitations. Everybody can change to live an inspired and WINNING life, and you are one of the ones who will do so.

Motivate yourself by taking the action steps you've written after each quote. If you desire more assistance, I'm here for you. You can email me at **coachwinn@ coachwinnspeaks.com.**

ACKNOWLEDGMENTS

There are not enough pages in a book to acknowledge all the people who have made a difference in my life. Some of you have written books, produced pod-casts, webinars or even television shows. Other have hugged me, supported me and loved me through challenges. To all of you, I send blessings and hugs.

Pam Winn
Darlene Chandler
Dr. Clarence Winn
Lauretta Yantis
Reita Clanton
Lynne Fitzgerald
Dr. Danny Brassell
Kathryn Roberts
James Malinchak
LaVonna Roth
Lila Larson
Kevin Clayson
Gary Barnes
Dr. Bren Stevens
Dr. Edward Welch
Oprah Winfrey
Dr. Wayne Dyer
Ellen DeGeneres
Eric Lambert
Cynthia Stinger
MaryPhyl Dwight
Forbes Riley
John Assaraf

Brian Tracy
Stephanie Fofonoff
Brene' Brown
Jane Krizek
David Otey
Laura
Morledge Anderson
Barb Clementi
Ashley Warren
Carlos Lopez
Trisha Glen
Dee Miller
Hillary Summers
Billings
Chamber of Commerce
Deborah
"Atianne" Wilson
Cary Veis
Stacy Birnbach
The Donaldson Family
Zig Ziglar
Jim Rohn
Donnette Roberts

Izabela Lundberg
Don Miguel Ruiz
John Maxwell
Deepak Chopra
Byron Katie
Chris Moat
Derek Dukes
MSU-Northern
Rachel Pike
University of Charleston
Penny Stone

USA Team Handball
Coke Lindsey
Anthony Robbins
Carmen Forest
Jack Canfield
All my former teammates
John Formica
Sandra Delariva Repede
Sheila Green Gerding
All of my former players

MOTIVATE AND INSPIRE OTHERS!

Share this Book!

THE WIN PHILOSOPHY QUOTE BOOK

You are limited by your ability to believe you can create, not by your ability to create. By reading one quote a day and applying the action steps you write down, you will discover your hidden potential. Imagine what you can accomplish once your mindset is stimulated to the right set point.

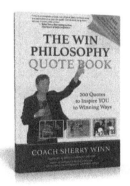

Retail $11.97

Special Quantity Discounts

10-20 Books	$8.00
21-99 Books	$7.00
100-299 Books	$6.00
299-499 Books	$5.00
500+ Books	$4.00